Use at least 11 of your spelling
all spelling words used in the st

Spelling Test

	Your Answers		**Correct Spelling If Incorrect**
1		1	
2		2	
3		3	
4		4	
5		5	
6		6	
7		7	
8		8	
9		9	
10		10	
11		11	
12		12	
13		13	
14		14	
15		15	
16		16	
17		17	
18		18	
19		19	
20		20	

Extra Credit Spelling Words Scramble

Name: _____

Date: _____

BONE	BREAD	BOOK	BREAK	BEWARE	BLOCK
BICYCLE	CLASSES	BIGGER	BRAKE	BROWN	CHANCE
BRICK					

1. AREEWB   _ _ _ _ R E   8. AEDRB   _ _ _ _ D

2. YLCBEIC   _ _ C _ _ _ E   9. BAKRE   B _ _ _ _

3. BEGRGI   _ _ _ G _ R   10. BRCKI   _ _ I _ _

4. LCOKB   _ L _ _ _   11. BWRNO   _ _ _ W _

5. OEBN   _ _ _ _   12. HNCECA   C _ A _ _ _

6. BOKO   _ O _ _   13. EASLSSC   _ L _ S _ _ _

7. KBEAR   _ _ _ _ E

Write sentences using words from above:

1. _____

2. _____

3. _____

4. _____

5. _____

Use at least 9 of your spelling words in a short creative story. Underline all spelling words used in the story.

Spelling Test

	Your Answers		**Correct Spelling If Incorrect**
1		1	
2		2	
3		3	
4		4	
5		5	
6		6	
7		7	
8		8	
9		9	
10		10	
11		11	
12		12	
13		13	
14		14	
15		15	
16		16	
17		17	
18		18	
19		19	
20		20	

Extra Credit Spelling Words Scramble

Name: _____

Date: _____

CRANE	CROWN	CUBE	CLOUD	DAISY	CONFUSE
COCOA	CLOWN	CLOSET	CROW	CLAW	CONFUSE
COACH					

1. ACLW   _ L _ _

2. SCOELT   C _ _ _ _ T

3. DCUOL   _ L _ _ _

4. CLNOW   _ _ _ W _

5. ACHOC   _ _ _ C _

6. COOAC   C _ _ _ _

7. ECSNUFO   _ _ _ _ U S _

8. ECUSONF   _ _ _ F _ _ E

9. RNECA   _ _ A _ _

10. OCRW   _ R _ _

11. RNCWO   C _ _ _ _

12. ECBU   C _ _ _

13. SAIYD   _ _ _ _ Y

Write sentences using words from above:

1. _____

2. _____

3. _____

4. _____

5. _____

Use at least 14 of your spelling words in a short creative story. Underline all spelling words used in the story.

Spelling Test

	Your Answers		**Correct Spelling If Incorrect**
1		1	
2		2	
3		3	
4		4	
5		5	
6		6	
7		7	
8		8	
9		9	
10		10	
11		11	
12		12	
13		13	
14		14	
15		15	
16		16	
17		17	
18		18	
19		19	
20		20	

Extra Credit Spelling Words Scramble

Name: _____

Date: _____

EIGHT	FAIR	FINE	EGGSHELL	EAST	DIVIDE
DOES	FLOUR	FOSSIL	FARE	FLAME	FLOWER
DOWNSPOUT	DISTANCE	FLAME			

1. CSDINAET   _ _ _ _ A N _ _

2. IDIVDE   D _ _ _ D _

3. DSEO   _ _ _ S

4. TSWODNPUO   D O _ _ _ _ _ _ _

5. ESAT   _ A _ _

6. LHELEGSG   _ G _ _ _ E _ _

7. GITEH   _ _ _ H _

8. IF AR   _ _ _ _

9. EFAR   _ _ _ E

10. FENI   _ _ N _

11. LMFEA   _ _ _ _ E

12. LEMFA   F _ _ _ _

13. UFOLR   _ L _ _ _

14. RLWFEO   _ _ O _ _ R

15. SOSILF   _ _ _ S _ L

Write sentences using words from above:

1. _____
2. _____
3. _____
4. _____
5. _____

Use at least 7 of your spelling words in a short creative story. Underline all spelling words used in the story.

Spelling Test

	Your Answers		**Correct Spelling If Incorrect**
1		1	
2		2	
3		3	
4		4	
5		5	
6		6	
7		7	
8		8	
9		9	
10		10	
11		11	
12		12	
13		13	
14		14	
15		15	
16		16	
17		17	
18		18	
19		19	
20		20	

Extra Credit Spelling Words Scramble

Name: _____

Date: _____

HOWEVER	HELLO	HOLLOW	LICENSE	INCH	FROG
KEPT	HOUND	GIVEN	GLOBE	LOLLIPOP	LINES
GRADE	LAUGH	IRON	HEIGHT	GRAPH	

1. ROFG   F _ _ _

2. VIGEN   _ _ _ _ N

3. OLGEB   _ _ O _ _

4. EGADR   _ _ _ _ E

5. PGRAH   _ _ _ _ H

6. HGEIHT   _ _ _ _ H T

7. LEHOL   H _ _ _ _

8. OLHOWL   H _ _ _ O _

9. OD NUH   _ O _ _ _

10. RVOHWEE   _ _ W _ _ _ R

11. CINH   _ _ _ H

12. ROIN   I _ _ _

13. KETP   _ _ P _

14. LUHGA   _ _ U _ _

15. ISNELEC   _ _ _ _ _ S E

16. LEISN   _ _ _ E _

17. LOILOLPP   _ _ _ _ I _ _ P

Write sentences using words from above:

1. _____

2. _____

3. _____

4. _____

5. _____

Use at least 8 of your spelling words in a short creative story. Underline all spelling words used in the story.

Spelling Test

	Your Answers		**Correct Spelling If Incorrect**
1		1	
2		2	
3		3	
4		4	
5		5	
6		6	
7		7	
8		8	
9		9	
10		10	
11		11	
12		12	
13		13	
14		14	
15		15	
16		16	
17		17	
18		18	
19		19	
20		20	

Extra Credit Spelling Words Scramble

Name: _____

Date: _____

OCTAGON	MEOW	PANCAKE	MOUTH	PANTS	MULTIPLY
OLIVE	OWN	NOTE	MEDAL	MANY	OATMEAL
METAL	OPTION	MAGICAL	MASK		

1. MCAILAG   M _ _ _ C _ _

2. AYMN   M _ _ _

3. KMSA   M _ _ _

4. DELMA   _ E _ _ _

5. WOME   _ E _ _

6. EATML   _ E _ _ _

7. HUTOM   _ _ _ T _

8. MLLPYTUI   _ _ _ T _ _ L _

9. OENT   _ O _ _

10. ELAMTOA   _ A _ _ _ A _

11. GCTNOOA   _ _ _ _ G O _

12. LOEIV   O _ _ _ _

13. IPOTNO   O _ _ _ _ N

14. WON   _ _ N

15. PEAANKC   _ _ _ _ A _ E

16. TNSAP   _ _ _ _ S

Write sentences using words from above:

1. _____

2. _____

3. _____

4. _____

5. _____

Use at least 12 of your spelling words in a short creative story. Underline all spelling words used in the story.

Spelling Test

	Your Answers		Correct Spelling If Incorrect
1		1	
2		2	
3		3	
4		4	
5		5	
6		6	
7		7	
8		8	
9		9	
10		10	
11		11	
12		12	
13		13	
14		14	
15		15	
16		16	
17		17	
18		18	
19		19	
20		20	

Extra Credit Spelling Words Scramble

Name: _____

Date: _____

RIVER	READING	PIECE	PLASTIC	RHYME	PEACHES
PILOT	REMEMBER	REACH	RAMP	PEACE	PLATE
RAISE	POWERFUL	REPLY	REUSE		

1. AEPEC   _ _ _ _ E

2. CPSHEEA   _ _ A C _ _ _

3. CEPEI   _ _ _ _ E

4. TPOIL   _ _ _ O _

5. LTCSIAP   _ L _ _ T _ _

6. LAETP   _ _ _ T _

7. RF POEULW   _ _ _ E _ _ U _

8. EASIR   _ _ I _ _

9. MPAR   _ _ _ P

10. EHC RA   _ E _ _ H

11. INERGAD   _ _ A D _ _ _

12. EREMREMB   R _ _ _ M _ _ _

13. YLREP   _ _ _ L _

14. EEUSR   _ E _ _ _

15. EMRYH   _ _ _ M _

16. IEVRR   _ _ V _ _

Write sentences using words from above:

1. _____

2. _____

3. _____

4. _____

5. _____

Use at least 10 of your spelling words in a short creative story. Underline all spelling words used in the story.

Spelling Test

	Your Answers
1	
2	
3	
4	
5	
6	
7	
8	
9	
10	
11	
12	
13	
14	
15	
16	
17	
18	
19	
20	

	Correct Spelling If Incorrect
1	
2	
3	
4	
5	
6	
7	
8	
9	
10	
11	
12	
13	
14	
15	
16	
17	
18	
19	
20	

Extra Credit Spelling Words Scramble

Name: _____

Date: _____

SMILE	SENTENCE	SERVICE	SHOUT	ROWDY	SAFETY
SEAS	SEES	SILENT	SEASON	SNOW	SKATE
SAIL	SOLD	SALE	SMILE	SENSE	ROSE

1. OERS   _ _ _ E
2. RWYDO   _ _ _ _ Y
3. YFETSA   _ _ _ E _ Y
4. IASL   _ A _ _
5. SAEL   _ A _ _
6. SASE   _ E _ _
7. NASOSE   _ _ A S _ _
8. S ESE   S _ _ _
9. ESSNE   _ _ _ S _

10. NEENSCET   _ _ N _ _ _ _ E
11. EREIVCS   _ _ _ _ I C _
12. HUTOS   _ H _ _ _
13. TNEILS   _ _ _ E N _
14. ATSKE   S _ _ _ _
15. ESIML   _ _ I _ _
16. IMLSE   _ _ _ _ E
17. O WSN   _ _ O _
18. OLDS   S _ _ _

Write sentences using words from above:

1. _____
2. _____
3. _____
4. _____
5. _____

Use at least 5 of your spelling words in a short creative story. Underline all spelling words used in the story.

Spelling Test

Your Answers	Correct Spelling If Incorrect
1	1
2	2
3	3
4	4
5	5
6	6
7	7
8	8
9	9
10	10
11	11
12	12
13	13
14	14
15	15
16	16
17	17
18	18
19	19
20	20

Extra Credit Spelling Words Scramble

Name: _____

Date: _____

TAP	THEY	STAMP	STRIPE	SPECIAL	TOWEL
STONE	THERE	TAPE	STATION	THEIR	SURROUND
SOUND	STAGE	SORRY	TELEPHONE	TRACK	

1. ORRY S   S _ R _ _   10. PTA   T _ _

2. OUDNS   _ _ U _ _   11. PETA   _ A _ _

3. AICPLSE   _ _ _ _ I A _   12. OENPTHLEE   T _ _ _ _ _ _ E

4. SAGET   _ _ A _ _   13. THIRE   T _ _ _ _

5. MPAST   S _ _ _ _   14. ERTEH   T _ _ _ _

6. ANTOITS   _ T _ _ I _ _   15. HEYT   _ H _ _

7. OESTN   _ _ O _ _   16. WOETL   _ _ _ _ L

8. TIEPSR   _ _ R _ P _   17. KTRCA   _ _ _ C _

9. RNOS UURD   _ _ R _ _ U _ _

Write sentences using words from above:

1. _____

2. _____

3. _____

4. _____

5. _____

Use at least 16 of your spelling words in a short creative story. Underline all spelling words used in the story.

Spelling Test

	Your Answers		**Correct Spelling If Incorrect**
1		1	
2		2	
3		3	
4		4	
5		5	
6		6	
7		7	
8		8	
9		9	
10		10	
11		11	
12		12	
13		13	
14		14	
15		15	
16		16	
17		17	
18		18	
19		19	
20		20	

Use at least 14 of your spelling words in a short creative story. Underline all spelling words used in the story.

Spelling Test

	Your Answers		Correct Spelling If Incorrect
1		1	
2		2	
3		3	
4		4	
5		5	
6		6	
7		7	
8		8	
9		9	
10		10	
11		11	
12		12	
13		13	
14		14	
15		15	
16		16	
17		17	
18		18	
19		19	
20		20	

Use at least 17 of your spelling words in a short creative story. Underline all spelling words used in the story.

Spelling Test

	Your Answers		**Correct Spelling If Incorrect**
1		1	
2		2	
3		3	
4		4	
5		5	
6		6	
7		7	
8		8	
9		9	
10		10	
11		11	
12		12	
13		13	
14		14	
15		15	
16		16	
17		17	
18		18	
19		19	
20		20	

Use at least 5 of your spelling words in a short creative story. Underline all spelling words used in the story.

Spelling Test

	Your Answers		**Correct Spelling If Incorrect**
1		1	
2		2	
3		3	
4		4	
5		5	
6		6	
7		7	
8		8	
9		9	
10		10	
11		11	
12		12	
13		13	
14		14	
15		15	
16		16	
17		17	
18		18	
19		19	
20		20	

Use at least 7 of your spelling words in a short creative story. Underline all spelling words used in the story.

Spelling Test

Your Answers		**Correct Spelling If Incorrect**
1		1
2		2
3		3
4		4
5		5
6		6
7		7
8		8
9		9
10		10
11		11
12		12
13		13
14		14
15		15
16		16
17		17
18		18
19		19
20		20

Use at least 12 of your spelling words in a short creative story. Underline all spelling words used in the story.

Spelling Test

	Your Answers
1	
2	
3	
4	
5	
6	
7	
8	
9	
10	
11	
12	
13	
14	
15	
16	
17	
18	
19	
20	

	Correct Spelling If Incorrect
1	
2	
3	
4	
5	
6	
7	
8	
9	
10	
11	
12	
13	
14	
15	
16	
17	
18	
19	
20	

Use at least 10 of your spelling words in a short creative story. Underline all spelling words used in the story.

Spelling Test

Your Answers		**Correct Spelling If Incorrect**
1		1
2		2
3		3
4		4
5		5
6		6
7		7
8		8
9		9
10		10
11		11
12		12
13		13
14		14
15		15
16		16
17		17
18		18
19		19
20		20

Use at least 8 of your spelling words in a short creative story. Underline all spelling words used in the story.

Spelling Test

	Your Answers
1	
2	
3	
4	
5	
6	
7	
8	
9	
10	
11	
12	
13	
14	
15	
16	
17	
18	
19	
20	

	Correct Spelling If Incorrect
1	
2	
3	
4	
5	
6	
7	
8	
9	
10	
11	
12	
13	
14	
15	
16	
17	
18	
19	
20	

Use at least 13 of your spelling words in a short creative story. Underline all spelling words used in the story.

Spelling Test

	Your Answers		Correct Spelling If Incorrect
1		1	
2		2	
3		3	
4		4	
5		5	
6		6	
7		7	
8		8	
9		9	
10		10	
11		11	
12		12	
13		13	
14		14	
15		15	
16		16	
17		17	
18		18	
19		19	
20		20	

Use at least 11 of your spelling words in a short creative story. Underline all spelling words used in the story.

Spelling Test

Your Answers		**Correct Spelling If Incorrect**
1		1
2		2
3		3
4		4
5		5
6		6
7		7
8		8
9		9
10		10
11		11
12		12
13		13
14		14
15		15
16		16
17		17
18		18
19		19
20		20

Use at least 9 of your spelling words in a short creative story. Underline all spelling words used in the story.

Spelling Test

	Your Answers		**Correct Spelling If Incorrect**
1		1	
2		2	
3		3	
4		4	
5		5	
6		6	
7		7	
8		8	
9		9	
10		10	
11		11	
12		12	
13		13	
14		14	
15		15	
16		16	
17		17	
18		18	
19		19	
20		20	

Use at least 15 of your spelling words in a short creative story. Underline all spelling words used in the story.

Use at least 11 of your spelling words in a short creative story. Underline all spelling words used in the story.

Spelling Test

	Your Answers		**Correct Spelling If Incorrect**
1		1	
2		2	
3		3	
4		4	
5		5	
6		6	
7		7	
8		8	
9		9	
10		10	
11		11	
12		12	
13		13	
14		14	
15		15	
16		16	
17		17	
18		18	
19		19	
20		20	

Use at least 9 of your spelling words in a short creative story. Underline all spelling words used in the story.

Spelling Test

Your Answers		**Correct Spelling If Incorrect**
1		1
2		2
3		3
4		4
5		5
6		6
7		7
8		8
9		9
10		10
11		11
12		12
13		13
14		14
15		15
16		16
17		17
18		18
19		19
20		20

Use at least 14 of your spelling words in a short creative story. Underline all spelling words used in the story.

Spelling Test

Your Answers		**Correct Spelling If Incorrect**
1.		1.
2.		2.
3.		3.
4.		4.
5.		5.
6.		6.
7.		7.
8.		8.
9.		9.
10.		10.
11.		11.
12.		12.
13.		13.
14.		14.
15.		15.
16.		16.
17.		17.
18.		18.
19.		19.
20.		20.

Made in the USA
Monee, IL
17 March 2020